# MOONSEED
## — AND —
# MISTLETOE

## A BOOK OF POISONOUS WILD PLANTS

# CAROL LERNER

Morrow Junior Books · New York

The author thanks Floyd Swink, Taxonomist of the Morton Arboretum in Lisle, Illinois, for reviewing the text of this book.

Printed in Hong Kong.
1  2  3  4  5  6  7  8  9  10
Library of Congress Cataloging-in-Publication Data
Lerner, Carol.
Moonseed and mistletoe.
Includes index.
Summary: Introduces plants to be found in the wild
that may be troublesome to us by irritating the skin or
causing illness or death from tasting or eating.
1. Poisonous plants—United States—Juvenile literature.
2. Poisonous plants—Canada—Juvenile literature.
[1. Poisonous plants]  I. Title.
QK100.U6L47 1987      581.6'9'0973      87-13989
ISBN 0-688-07307-7
ISBN 0-688-07308-5 (lib. bdg.)

# CONTENTS

# Introduction

Today most of us grow up knowing little or nothing about the wild plants and animals of the countryside. We live in cities or suburbs. When we visit the woods or the fields, we come as strangers. The names of the things around us there and their ways of living are a mystery.

When most Americans still lived as country people, the wild plants were a part of everyday life. Some were eaten as food; others were used to make home medicines. A number of the "poisonous" plants in this book were the very ones used in those herbal medicines. Taken in the wrong amount, the same plant can be a poison instead of a cure.

In fact, a surprising number of our wild plants do contain poisons in their juices. Many of these plants are very common, and some grow in waste places around our homes. Over 700 different species in the United States and Canada are known to have caused illness.

Of course, not every poisonous plant is deadly. Some plants that are called "poisonous" simply cause skin rashes from touching them. A few common ones are described in the first chapter, but there are many more. You may be bothered by a few or many or none of these plants. For most people who are sensitive to them, it's just an unpleasant experience: They don't need the doctor, and the rash passes away in a week or so. Some people, however, do get very sick, especially if the plant touches a large area of skin, or if the person touched is unusually sensitive to the chemical in that particular plant.

Plants that irritate the skin are the only ones that are likely to cause you trouble in the wild—unless, of course, you taste wild plants without knowing they are safe.

People do taste without knowing. Each year, poison control centers receive thousands of calls about possible poisonings from eating plants. Most often the calls concern very young children below school age.

In *Moonseed and Mistletoe*, there is room for only a few of the many poisonous plants that grow wild in the United States and Canada. (The names of the plants in the color illustrations appear in capital letters when they are first discussed.) Since all the examples here are flowering plants, mushrooms and ferns are not included. Some very poisonous tropical plants that grow only in southern Florida were also omitted in favor of those that grow in our more typical climates.

All of the plants in this book are found in places where no one has planted them. Some are natives that grew here before Europeans came to America. Some are weeds from other continents that the explorers and settlers brought with them. A number began as garden plants but have spread to uncultivated places.

When choosing the examples, I looked for plants that are actually on record as causing people to become sick. Many plants that are not here could also cause illness. If they haven't, it is because people are not tempted to eat them. The cockleburs, for example, are common weeds that grow in all parts of the country. The seeds are poisonous, but they grow as part of a spiny bur that no one would put in the mouth.

Enjoying plants is one of the pleasures of being in the outdoors. They are interesting and often beautiful. If you follow a few rules, nothing should spoil that pleasure. Learn to recognize the plants that might be harmful if you touch them. Don't taste any wild plant unless you know positively that it is safe, and unless you are absolutely sure that it is the plant you think it is.

*Moonseed and Mistletoe* introduces a handful of plants that can be troublesome. Although it gives some warnings about poisonous plants that resemble edible ones, it is not a guide for collecting wild food. Anyone who wants to experiment with wild foods needs a good field guide that tells—in clear detail—how to recognize the safe plants and how to tell them apart from any poisonous look-alikes.

## Chapter One
# TOUCH-ME-NOTS

No wild plants bring misery to more people than POISON IVY and POISON OAK. At least half of us get red and burning skin, and then itching and blisters, after we touch one of these plants.

Poison oak and ivy contain the same poison—a gummy juice that is inside every part of the plants. It can't hurt anyone as long as it stays there, but when a leaf is bent or torn—or even if an insect cuts a tiny hole in a leaf or stem—the poison comes to the surface. It is so strong that the amount on a pinhead can give a rash to five hundred people. And it has a long life: Scientists got skin rashes from touching a dry plant sample that was one hundred years old.

A hand can spread the poison to other parts of the body. Even someone who has never been near poison oak or ivy can get the poison from another person's hand, or from a dog or a tool that has rubbed against one of these plants.

The plants are most dangerous when they burn, for then the poison rises in tiny drops along with the smoke and ashes. Breathing this smoke hurts the lungs and can kill. *Never* put poison ivy or poison oak into a fire.

One or both of these plants can be found in every state of the United States except Alaska and Hawaii. Poison ivy grows over most of the country and into Canada and Mexico. Western poison oak is found along the Pacific Coast, as far north as British Columbia; an eastern species grows in the southeastern quarter of the United States.

Poison oak and ivy are alike in many ways. They may grow as a low ground plant or as a bush. Western poison oak and poison ivy are often climbing vines. Their flowers are small and greenish, the fruits dull white, hanging in clusters. The leaves have three separate parts or leaflets, but the shapes of the leaflets are not always the same. They may have one or more lobes that stick out like thumbs on a mitten. Other plants have leaves with several smaller teeth along the edges or with smooth edges. It's a good idea to learn what poison ivy (or poison oak) looks like in the place where you live.

FOUR POISON IVY LEAVES, SHOWING A VARIETY OF SHAPES
*(leaves 4″–14″)*

Not every plant with a three-part leaf is a threat, of course. Wild strawberry and many of the wild raspberries and blackberries also carry leaves in groups of three. The leaf edges of all these plants have many small, sharp teeth. Fragrant sumac, a bush that grows from Quebec to Texas, has a leaf like poison ivy, but the sumac leaf does not have a bare stem between the two lower leaflets and the end one.

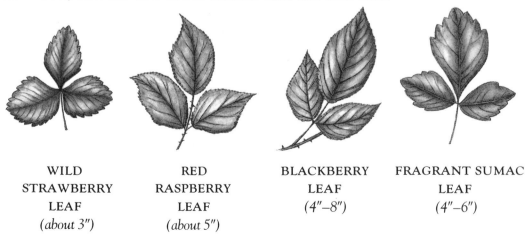

WILD
STRAWBERRY
LEAF
*(about 3″)*

RED
RASPBERRY
LEAF
*(about 5″)*

BLACKBERRY
LEAF
(4″–8″)

FRAGRANT SUMAC
LEAF
(4″–6″)

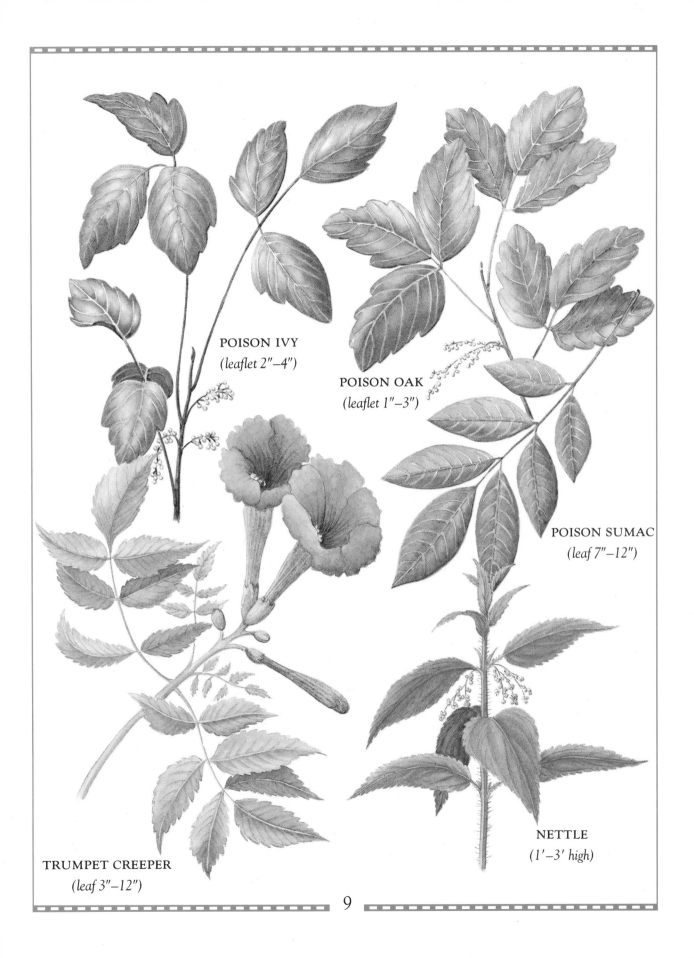

POISON IVY
*(leaflet 2″–4″)*

POISON OAK
*(leaflet 1″–3″)*

POISON SUMAC
*(leaf 7″–12″)*

TRUMPET CREEPER
*(leaf 3″–12″)*

NETTLE
*(1′–3′ high)*

POISON SUMAC is a close relative of poison oak and ivy and has the same poison. It grows in bogs and swamps, as a bush or small tree, in the eastern half of the United States and in a few areas in southern Canada near the Great Lakes. Its leaf might be confused with those of harmless sumacs that grow along forest edges and roadsides. Only one of these—dwarf sumac—has leaflets with smooth edges like the poison plants, but dwarf sumac can be identified by the "wing" on its stem between the leaflets.

POISON
SUMAC LEAF
*(7"–12")*
*5–13 leaflets*

STAGHORN
SUMAC LEAF
*(12"–24")*
*11–31 leaflets*

SMOOTH
SUMAC LEAF
*(10"–12")*
*11–31 leaflets*

DWARF
SUMAC LEAF
*(up to 12")*
*7–17 leaflets*

All the plants described so far are pests, but TRUMPET CREEPER is one that you can love or hate. Hummingbirds love the orange or red flowers. Gardeners choose it because it grows into a thick climbing plant loaded with bright blossoms. But trumpet creeper, also called cow itch, causes skin trouble, too. Some people get rashes and blisters from its leaves and flowers.

In the southeastern states, trumpet creeper grows in woods and along stream banks, and it spreads from there into farmers' fields and roadsides. Farther north and west, it escapes from gardens into woods and waste places. Once it starts growing, the creeper is there to stay. Even when its deep roots are cut, they sprout and grow new plants.

NETTLES are pest plants, but they, too, have their friends. Some kind of stinging nettle grows in most parts of North America. They are low plants of woods, roadsides, and waste places, with stems and leaves covered by fine hairs. Each hair is really a tiny hollow needle. When a bare leg or hand brushes against it, the needle shoots a chemical into the skin that causes stinging and burning. With most people, the sensation passes away within an hour.

NETTLE NEEDLES
ON A LEAF
*(enlarged)*

But nettles are favorites of many people who like to eat wild foods. They search out young plants and (using gloves!) gather the tops. After cooking, the plants can be eaten as a green vegetable. They taste something like spinach and are rich in vitamin C. However, some people are sensitive even to well-cooked nettles and feel the stinging in their throats after eating them.

## Chapter Two
# BEAUTIFUL BERRIES

Many wild fruits are good to eat. When you're walking through the forest, it's fun to pull off a ripe blackberry and pop it into your mouth. But some woodland fruits have dangerous look-alikes growing right beside them. *It is essential to know about a plant before you take a sample!*

LEAF OF
HIGHBUSH
BLUEBERRY
*(actual size)*

The seeds of BLUE COHOSH (COE-hahsh) look like blueberries. This plant grows in lush woods in the eastern half of the United States and northward into bordering parts of southeastern Canada. Its spring flowers are small, dull, and green-colored, but by late summer the plants hold seeds wrapped in a beautiful blue covering. Although these poisonous "berries" are bitter, some children have eaten them and then suffered severe stomach pains. The cohosh leaf is made up of many leaflets on a branching stalk, and most of the leaflets have lobes, or "thumbs," that stick out on one or both sides. They are very different from the smooth-edged leaves on all kinds of blueberry plants.

Two kinds of forest vines have fruits that are confused with wild grapes, and both have been blamed in the deaths of children. VIRGINIA CREEPER, or American woodbine, is a very common plant in eastern and central North America. Dark blue fruit grows in clusters on red stalks, and songbirds eat them without harm. But in an experiment, a guinea pig died after eating just twelve of these berries.

BLUE COHOSH
*(1'–3' high)*

VIRGINIA
CREEPER
*(leaf 3"–8")*

BITTERSWEET
NIGHTSHADE
*(leaf 1¹/₂"–4")*

MOONSEED
*(leaf 5"–11")*

WHITE BANEBERRY
*(1'–2' high)*

MAYAPPLE
*(1'–1¹/₂' high)*

You can recognize Virginia creeper by its five-part leaf: Each of the five parts is separate from the others except at the point where it attaches to the leaf stem. While some wild grapes have leaves with lobes and deep cuts between the lobes, the lobes are part of a single leaf surface.

GRAPE LEAF
*(3″–6″ wide)*

SEED OF A
MOONSEED
FRUIT
*(enlarged)*

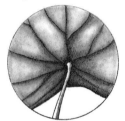

BACK OF A
MOONSEED LEAF
*(actual size)*

MOONSEED vine is less common than Virginia creeper, but it grows in some of the same woodlands in eastern and central North America. Moonseed vine also bears dark fruits that look like small grapes. Each of these has a single large seed, shaped like the moon when it is nearly full, while a wild grape has several round seeds inside each fruit. Moonseed can be told apart from grape by its unusual leaf: The leafstalk attaches to the underside of the moonseed leaf on the flat portion of the leaf, rather than at the very edge of it.

Some berries are unlike any fruits we know, but people eat them anyway, just because they look good enough to eat. Among these are the forest plants called baneberry. (The word "bane" means deadly poison.) WHITE BANEBERRY, or doll's-eyes, grows in the East and the Midwest. It has bright white fruits growing on thick red stalks. Each has a single dark spot—the "eye" of the doll.

Two species of red baneberry, a close relative, grow in woodlands in most of the United States except the far Southeast and in all of Canada except the most northern parts. They look like white baneberry but usually have red fruit. All parts of these plants are poisonous, and eating just a few of the berries can cause illness.

Some wild berries are safe only when they are completely ripe. The trouble comes when people do not recognize unripe fruits, or do not know their danger.

MAYAPPLE is a common wildflower of the eastern forests, and its big umbrella-like leaves are easy to spot. The fruit is a single large berry that looks like a small lime until it ripens and turns yellow. The unripe fruits, their seeds, and all other parts of the plant can make you sick. Even ripe fruits can cause stomach pains if eaten in large amounts.

Several kinds of nightshade grow all over the United States and in Canada, Mexico, and farther south. Some are native plants; others are weeds that came from Europe, South America, or elsewhere; still other members of the group (potato and eggplant) are grown as food crops.

**HORSE NETTLE**
*(8″–32″ high)*

Black nightshade grows in the eastern half of the United States and in the far West. Two other weedy nightshades are also widespread across North America in fields and roadsides, and in city parks and vacant lots as well. BITTERSWEET NIGHT-SHADE, also called climbing nightshade, grows as a low plant or as a sprawling vine, with clusters of green and ripening red berries. Horse nettle is a low prickly plant with larger fruits—about half an inch across—that turn yellow or orange.

It is certain that the berries of all these weedy nightshades can be deadly if eaten before they are entirely ripe. It is not certain that even the ripe berries of most of these plants are safe.

NIGHTSHADE
FLOWER
*(enlarged)*

You can recognize nightshade plants by their flowers. There are five petals, either white or purple, which turn back from the center of the nightshade flower. The center is a yellow cone formed by the stamens.

## *Chapter Three*
# DON'T EAT THE WILDFLOWERS

Any part of a plant may be dangerous. Flowers, leaves, stems, and roots have all been causes of human poisoning. Often someone confuses a poisonous plant with a useful one and brings it home. In the past, people using homemade herbal medicines were often the victims of these mistakes. Today it might be someone eating wild food plants.

The carrot family contains a huge number of different plants. Some of them are deadly. As in many human families, the various members often have a strong resemblance to each other.

WATER HEMLOCKS are among the most poisonous wild plants in North America. One or more species can be found in wet fields and swampy ground all over the United States and Canada. These are tall plants with big hollow stems and flat-topped clusters of many small white flowers. Fat little roots, looking like a bunch of white carrots, grow attached to the bottom of the stem.

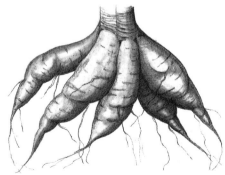

WATER HEMLOCK ROOTS
*(1"–4" long)*

People dig and eat these roots, thinking they are wild parsnips. In fact, they are the most poisonous part of the plant. As little as one mouthful or one small root can kill. Other parts are dangerous, too: Children can be poisoned by using peashooters or whistles made from the plant's hollow stem.

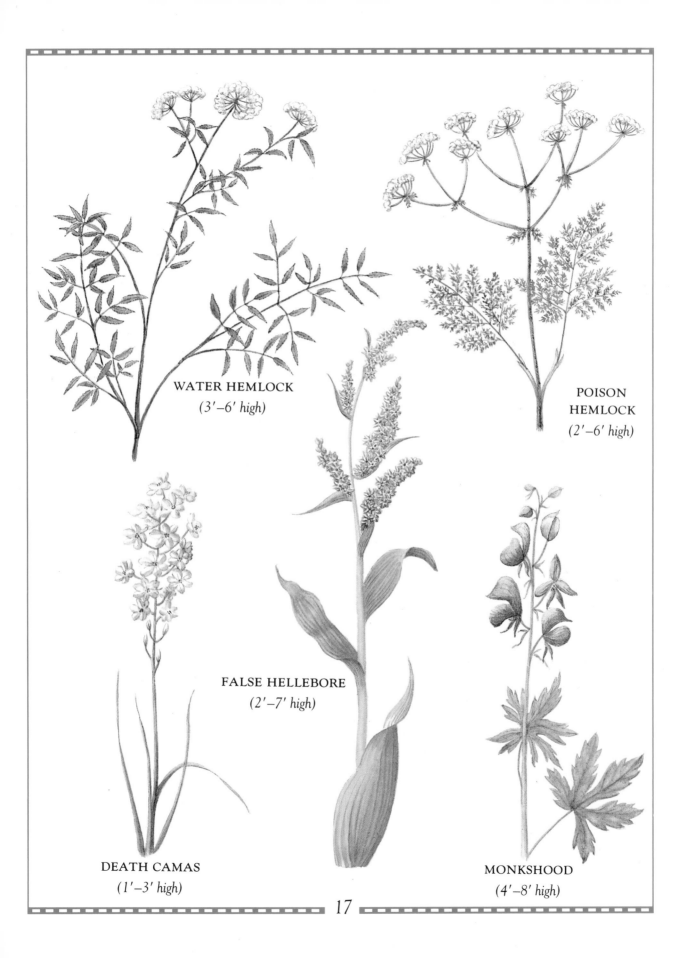

WATER HEMLOCK
*(3'–6' high)*

POISON
HEMLOCK
*(2'–6' high)*

FALSE HELLEBORE
*(2'–7' high)*

DEATH CAMAS
*(1'–3' high)*

MONKSHOOD
*(4'–8' high)*

DETAIL OF A
POISON
HEMLOCK LEAF
*(actual size)*

POISON HEMLOCK, in the same family, has a similar poison. This plant came over from Europe and now grows as a weed in waste places. It is found throughout most of the United States and in eastern Canada and British Columbia. Eating any part can cause illness or even death. In European folktales, it is one of the plants listed in recipes for witches' brews. It resembles water hemlock, but its leaflets are smaller. People mistake the leaves for parsley or gather the seeds, thinking they are anise.

The lilies are another large group of plants with a few family members that can make people deathly sick. Some lilies have underground bulbs that are good to eat. About fifteen different species of a plant called DEATH CAMAS grow in fields and woodlands around the United States and across Canada. These bulbs are definitely not safe to eat.

DEATH CAMAS BULB
*(actual size)*

Since early times, the bulbs of a completely different wild plant also called camas have been used as food. Most human poisonings from eating death camas bulbs are the result of confusing the poisonous plants with the edible ones. Edible camas bulbs were an important food for American Indians and they knew the plants well, but even they sometimes ate death camas bulbs by mistake.

Both kinds of plants have six-part flowers, narrow leaves that are almost like grass, and small bulbs.

FALSE HELLEBORE is another poisonous lily. One or more species of this plant can be found in most parts of North America except on the Great Plains and in the most northern parts of Canada. False hellebores can be recognized by the deep folds or pleats running side by side down the length of their large leaves.

They sometimes grow in the same wet fields and woods where skunk cabbage is found, and the two kinds of plants look much alike when they are young. People gathering young skunk cabbage leaves to cook as a vegetable have mistakenly used young shoots of false hellebore instead. Skunk cabbage does not have the same pattern of long, parallel leaf veins, but this is not obvious when the shoots are collected before the leaves have unrolled. As the leaf grows, the difference in vein pattern is clear.

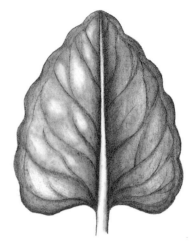

SKUNK CABBAGE LEAF
*(12"–24")*

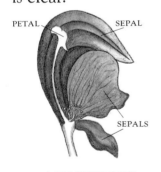

MONKSHOOD
FLOWER
*(enlarged)*
*cut open to show petal*

Another deadly plant, called MONKSHOOD, is in the buttercup family. It gets its name from the large sepal that covers the flower like a hood. Sepals are the parts of a flower that grow outside the petals and cover the bud before it opens. Most sepals are green and smaller than the petals of a fully opened flower, but monkshood sepals are blue, purple, yellow, or white and look like petals. The real petals are much smaller and are hidden within the large sepals.

Several wild species of monkshood grow in woodlands and along mountain streams in the eastern United States. Another is found in mountains and meadows of the West, from California and New Mexico to British Columbia and Alaska. The thick rootstock has sometimes been mistaken for a

MONKSHOOD
ROOT
*(2 1/2" long)*

horseradish, even though the two plants are completely unlike. Eating the root can bring death in a few hours.

Even perfectly good food plants cause trouble if they are not prepared in the right way. POKEWEED is one of the best-known wild foods. It grows in woods and fields of southeastern Canada and in the eastern half of the United States. In the southern states, it is sold in stores as a vegetable. Each spring, thick young shoots push up from the big pokeweed root. The shoots must be boiled in several changes of cooking water to get rid of the poison.

YOUNG POKEWEED SHOOTS
*(6″–8″ high)*

Over the summer, the pokeweed plant may grow six feet tall or more. Its thick purple stems have spikes of small white flowers that turn into shiny dark berries. Every part of this plant is dangerous to eat then, because the poison becomes stronger as the plant grows. People get sick from pokeweed if they don't cook it enough, or if they pull up some root and eat that along with the leaf shoots, or if they eat the plant after it has grown too big to be safe.

Of course, cows, sheep, and other grazing animals spend a lot more time nibbling on wildflowers than people do. Much of what we know about dangerous plants comes from the experience of farmers who have seen livestock become sick. Yet the wild plant that has killed the most people in this country is one that cows—and not people—eat.

In the eighteenth and nineteenth centuries, farm families and sometimes whole towns fell ill with what was called "milk sickness." Most cases were in North Carolina, Indiana, Illinois, and Ohio, and even there the sickness only struck in some areas. Up to one-fourth of

**POKEWEED**
*(4'–10' high)*

**WHITE
SNAKEROOT**
*(1'–5' high)*

**JIMSONWEED**
*(2'–5' high)*

**YELLOW JESSAMINE**
*(leaf 1"–2¹/₂")*

the victims died, and those who lived needed several years to get back to full health again.

The sickness was finally traced back to a plant called WHITE SNAKE-ROOT. This is a weedy plant of open woodlands, clearings, and fields in the eastern and central states. It usually grows three or four feet tall, and in late summer or fall it blooms with clusters of tiny white flowers.

When a cow eats white snakeroot, the poison in the plant passes from the animal into her milk. In the days when all the milk came from the family cow, an animal that ate enough snakeroot could make the whole household sick. Today milk from hundreds of different cows is mixed together before it is sold, and this kind of poisoning could not happen.

OPEN
"THORN APPLE"
(2") showing seeds
inside

Although people do not graze on wild plants, they do sometimes sample them out of simple curiosity. Even a taste of some plants is enough to bring illness or death. JIMSONWEED, or thorn apple, is another of the black-sheep members of the plant family that contains the nightshades. Several different species are found across North America. They grow tall, with trumpet-shaped flowers that are white or purplish. Children have become sick from sucking on the big flowers, but most often it is the small dark seeds inside the "thorn apple" that they eat. Just a few of these are enough to kill a child.

In spite of the fact that the dangers of jimsonweed are well known, people have tried to use them to grow food. The jimsonweed is not troubled by certain pests in the soil that attack tomato plants. Since tomatoes are in the same plant family, people thought they could make a better tomato plant by grafting tomato branches onto jimsonweed rootstocks. The parts soon grow together and become a single plant. However, while some of the tomatoes from these experiments were harmless, others were filled with poison made in the roots and sent up through all parts of the plant.

Another attractive funnel-shaped flower grows on YELLOW JESSA-MINE, a vine of the South. It attracts bees, and sometimes children pick the flowers to suck out the sweet nectar. Both children and young bees have been poisoned by the nectar, and a report from the last century tells of three adults who died after eating honey made from its flowers.

## Chapter Four

# A FOREST OF TROUBLES:
# POISONS IN BUSHES AND TREES

Many bushes belonging to the heath family are also popular as plantings around homes. Although this family includes the very edible blueberry and cranberry, some of the other heaths are beautiful flowering shrubs containing poison. Merely sucking on the flowers is enough to make a child sick. Honey made from them is both bitter and poisonous, and teas from the leaves or twigs can seriously raise or lower the blood pressure. Among the common poisonous bushes are mountain laurel and the rhododendrons.

MOUNTAIN LAUREL is a broad-leaved evergreen with clusters of pink or white flowers. It is native in the eastern mountains of the United States but is widely used in gardens. Other kinds of laurel shrubs grow in meadows and bogs, both in the East and in the West.

RHODODENDRON (roe-doe-DEN-dron) bushes also belong to the heaths and have the same poison as the laurels. Like the mountain laurel, they grow in cool mountain areas, but because of their beautiful flowers they are often planted in gardens wherever weather conditions make it possible to grow them.

BUCKEYE
SEED
*(actual size)*

One source of human poisoning from trees has been the large seeds of several common species. Buckeye and horse chestnut seeds are especially attractive to children: They are big, brown, and waxy-smooth, and they feel good in the hand.

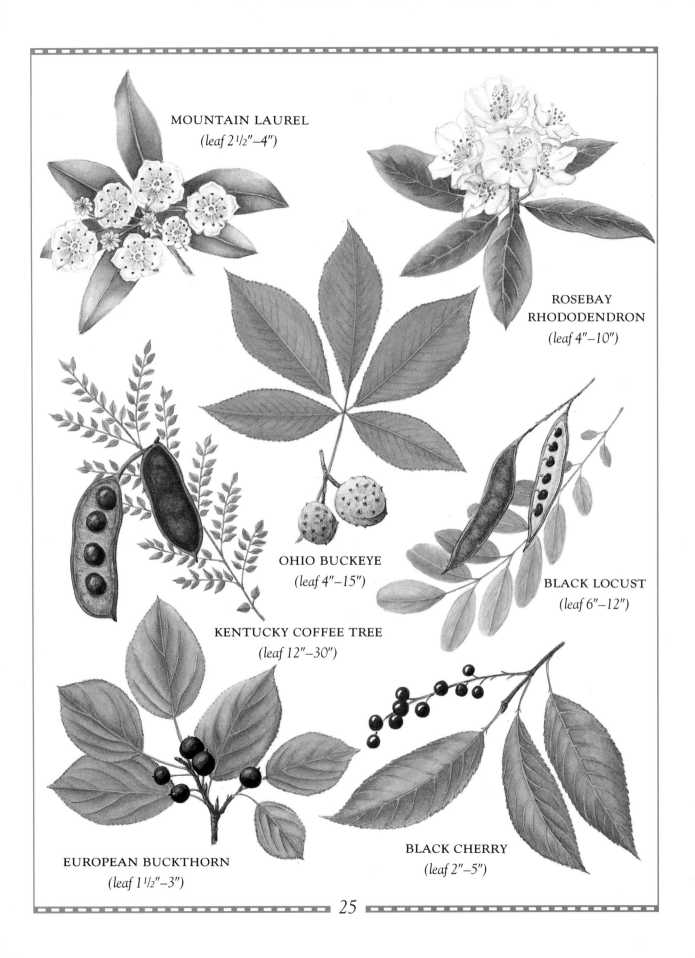

MOUNTAIN LAUREL
*(leaf 2¹/₂″–4″)*

ROSEBAY
RHODODENDRON
*(leaf 4″–10″)*

OHIO BUCKEYE
*(leaf 4″–15″)*

BLACK LOCUST
*(leaf 6″–12″)*

KENTUCKY COFFEE TREE
*(leaf 12″–30″)*

EUROPEAN BUCKTHORN
*(leaf 1¹/₂″–3″)*

BLACK CHERRY
*(leaf 2″–5″)*

BUCKEYES are woodland trees or bushes in the eastern United States and in the mountains of the Pacific Coast. The horse chestnut planted in city streets and parks is a related species that came from Europe.

HUSK OF AN
EDIBLE CHESTNUT
*(2"–2½")*

All parts of these plants contain poison. People used to throw crushed leaves and branches of buckeye into fishponds and then pick up the stunned fish from the water. But it is the seeds that usually cause human poisoning. Although they look like chestnuts, the husks of edible chestnuts are much more thickly covered by prickles. Leaves on the edible chestnut tree are single, while buckeyes and horse chestnuts have leaves made up of five to seven leaflets attached to the stem at a single point.

Since both trees are in the pea family, seeds of the Kentucky coffee tree and black locust grow like peas in a pod. The KENTUCKY COFFEE TREE is found in the Great Lakes states and in the central and south-central United States. The bitter "beans" grow in broad thick pods four to eight inches long. Although early settlers tried to make a drink like coffee from the beans, people have been known to become sick from eating the seeds and the sticky pulp that surrounds them inside the pod.

All parts of the BLACK LOCUST are said to be poisonous (though one popular writer on wild foods suggests frying and eating the flowers!). At one time, the black locust was a tree of the Southeast, but by now it has spread over most of the United States and to parts of Canada. It often forms thickets in old fields and waste places. Its pods are three or four inches long and hold a row of small brown seeds.

Some common woody plants used in foods and medicines are also known to contain poisons. BUCKTHORNS grow as bushes or small trees, and one or more kinds can be found in most parts of the United States and in the southern part of Canada. Species from Europe and Asia that were planted in gardens have also spread into the wild. Their fruits can be mistaken for wild cherries unless you look inside: A buckthorn fruit has two to four seeds, while a cherry has one.

Several kinds of buckthorn are used to make laxatives. The best known of these is the cascara tree of the Pacific Northwest. Its bark has been used for this purpose at least since the time of the early Spanish explorers. But eating the fruits or chewing on the bark of most buckthorn species can make you sick.

A more dangerous chemical is in the bark, leaves, and seeds of the wild cherry tree: After it is eaten, it turns into deadly cyanide inside the body. Even though children have been poisoned by chewing on its twigs, bark from the wild BLACK CHERRY is used in some herb teas. The cherries themselves are safe to eat—but the pits are not.

## Chapter Five

# DECK THE HALLS

Some of our wild plants keep their leaves and bright fruits long after the growing season has ended. In the fall and winter—and especially during the holiday season—we bring them inside to add color and cheer to our homes. But a few of these welcome plants also carry a hidden load of poisons. Once again, the berries—or berry-like fruits—are the most dangerous because they are the part most likely to be eaten. All of these plants should be placed out of the reach of very young children.

Bunches of BITTERSWEET are sold for indoor decoration every fall, and clusters of its fruit show up in many dry plant arrangements. Some of this bittersweet is collected from a native plant that grows as a climbing vine or a bush. Another kind of bittersweet, brought in from Asia, has escaped from gardens and now grows in the wild, too.

AMERICAN BITTERSWEET LEAVES (2"–4 1/4")

Bittersweet drops its leaves in fall but holds on to the fruits. As the plant dries, each fruit splits open to show the bright red seed covering within. All parts of the plant, including the fruit, are suspected of being poisonous.

Both holly and mistletoe come with a long history in European folklore and superstition. In more recent centuries, holly was turned into a Christian symbol, and it is a favorite evergreen of Christmastime. American holly is much like the European plant. Only branches from female trees have the bright red fruits among the dark leaves.

HOLLY
*(leaf 2"–4")*

MISTLETOE
*(leaf 1"–2")*

BITTERSWEET
*(nearly life size)*

HOLLY is one of the plants that are poisonous in some parts but not in others. The leaves are probably nonpoisonous, and, in fact, those of some native holly species were used by early settlers in the southeastern states to make teas. In any case, holly leaves—with sharp spines along the edges—are not very likely to be put into the mouth. But the berries do have poison: Twenty to thirty might be enough to cause death.

MISTLETOE
"ROOTS"
*(enlarged)*
*growing into*
*a tree branch*

In past centuries, MISTLETOE was considered a mystery. For one thing, it grows upon other plants. It is usually found far above the ground in the branches of oaks and other kinds of trees. For another, it steals from the plant that holds it. Mistletoe grows right into the wood of the host tree and uses some of the water and minerals it finds there. And something else: In winter, the plant keeps both leaves and fruit.

Mistletoe is also a poisonous plant. The fruits can make people sick, and the stems and leaves contain poison as well. But the magic that people believed was in mistletoe had nothing to do with its poison. A bit of this plant hung around the neck was supposed to protect against insects, sickness, and even witches! We still remember that tradition at New Year's time when we hang a sprig over the doorway. We are borrowing some of the magic of ancient times, when a stem of waxy green could keep evils from the doorstep all through the coming year.

# INDEX

The scientific names of these plants are shown in *italics*.
The illustrations appear in **boldface.**